ENDANGERED!

PARROTS

Casey Horton

Series Consultant: James G. Doherty
General Curator, The Bronx Zoo, New York

BENCHMARK BOOKS

MARSHALL CAVENDISH

NEW YORK

Benchmark Books
Marshall Cavendish Corporation
99 White Plains Road
Tarrytown, New York 10591-9001

Library of Congress Cataloging-in-Publication Data

Horton, Casey.
    Parrots / Casey Horton.
       p.   cm. — (Endangered!)
    Includes bibliographical references (p.   ) and index.
    Summary: An introduction to the parrot family, including physical
descriptions and habits of macaws, New Zealand parrots, and thick-
billed parrots.
    ISBN 0-7614-0222-5 (lib. bdg.)
    1. Parrots—Juvenile literature.   2. Endangered species—Juvenile
literature.   [1. Parrots. 2. Endangered species.]   I. Title.
II. Series.
QL696.P7H685 1996
598.71—dc20   95-39908
                                                     CIP
                                                      AC

Printed in Hong Kong

PICTURE CREDITS
*The publishers would like to thank the following picture libraries for supplying
the photographs used in this book:* Ardea 22; Bruce Coleman 4, 8, 9, 10, 11,
13, 24, 25, BC; Frank Lane Picture Agency (FLPA) 5, 6, 7, 14, 16, 17, 19, 20,
21, 23; FLPA/Silvestris FC; FLPA/Sunset 1, 12, 15; Natural History
Photographic Agency 26, 29; World Parrot Trust 27, 28.

Series created by Brown Packaging

Front cover: Hyacinth macaw.
Title page: Kakapo.
Back cover: Green-winged and scarlet macaws.

Contents

The white cockatoo is sometimes known as the umbrella cockatoo because of the way its crest of wide feathers fans out. Cockatoos can live to be 80 years old in zoos, and one may even have reached 120!

In the wild, parrots live mainly in **tropical** areas, but because people like to keep them as pets, many have been captured and sold all over the world. Unfortunately, too many are being trapped, leaving too few in the wild. This has happened to white cockatoos in Indonesia. Like all cockatoos, these birds have exotic crests of feathers on their heads and can be great "talkers." They can even be trained to do tricks, such as "shaking hands" with their feet and bowing to greet visitors. All this makes these parrots very popular as pets. **Conservationists** believe that as many as 7500 white cockatoos were caught in 1991 alone.

Parrots also suffer when people cut down forests, where many of them make their home. One species, the Queen of

Bavaria's conure, is in serious trouble. A beautiful golden bird with green wing feathers, this conure lives in a part of the Amazon **rainforest** of South America where two enormous highways have been built. To build these roads, millions of acres of forest had to be cleared, leaving many of these parrots without large trees to feed and nest in. At least one large dam has been built in the bird's **range** as well. Dams flood much of the surrounding countryside, killing the trees and putting these beautiful birds at risk.

In this book we will look at a number of species of parrots and learn how they live and why each of them is in danger. We will start with some of the largest and most beautiful – the macaws.

Queen of Bavaria's conures are beautiful to look at and are affectionate as pets, but they can make a tremendous amount of noise!

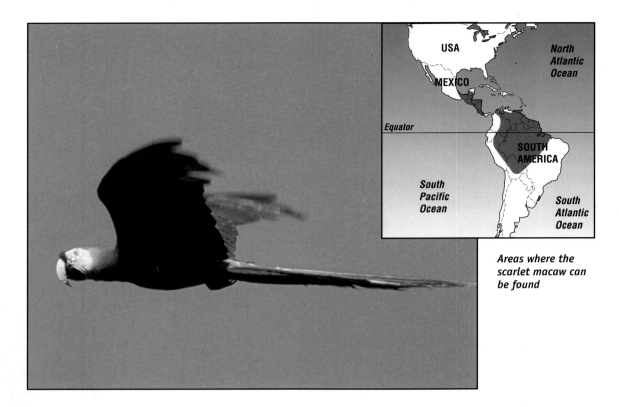

Areas where the scarlet macaw can be found

Macaws

Macaws live in the northern half of South America, in Central America, and in Mexico. Europeans once thought that they came from the island of Macao, near China, and that is how they got their name. Macaws are between 14 and 39 inches (36-100 cm) long, and there are 16 species.

Among the most striking of the macaws is the scarlet macaw. The scarlet macaw spends its life in the forests of Mexico, Central America, and northern South America, where it feeds mainly on fruit and nuts. Often, though, scarlet macaws can be seen at special cliffs, biting off lumps of clay and eating them. Some scientists think that

A scarlet macaw in flight. Scarlet macaws are sometimes killed for their tail feathers. These are turned into costumes for local dancers.

the parrots' usual diet may contain poisons and that the clay contains natural remedies that the macaws need to remain healthy. The problem is that **birds of prey** can see the parrots easily against the cliffs, and human hunters also go there to trap the birds for sale as pets.

Unlike the multi-colored scarlet macaw, most macaws are mainly one color. Blue macaws, for example, are pretty much blue all over. At one time, there were four species of

Scarlet and green-winged macaws at a clay cliff. The scarlet macaws have yellow patches on their wings.

blue macaws; today, there are only three. One of them, Spix's macaw, has almost disappeared in the wild, mainly because of trapping. At the end of 1994, only one wild bird survived, so it had no chance of finding a **mate**. Scientists released a **captive** bird near where the survivor was living in northeastern Brazil. It seems that the two birds have paired up, and scientists hope they will be able to breed.

The largest of all parrots is the hyacinth macaw. This magnificent bird is 39 inches (1 m) long – about the length of a baseball bat. It is deep blue all over and lives in Brazil and in parts of Bolivia and Paraguay. Like most macaws it makes its home in the forest, although it is also found on **savannas** (grasslands with scattered trees).

The last wild Spix's macaw. Since the photograph was taken, this lonely bird has been given a companion.

Area where the hyacinth macaw can be found

Besides its size, the hyacinth macaw is remarkable for its amazingly strong bill. The macaw needs this because its favorite foods are hard-shelled palm nuts. Macaws pick these nuts up off the ground after they have fallen from the trees. To get at the soft part inside, a macaw grasps a nut with its foot, then uses its bill to crack it open.

The hyacinth is another macaw that people like to keep as a pet. Trappers have taken huge numbers of them from the wild. As long ago as the 1970s, the Brazilian government made it illegal to export all birds. Then in the 1980s, many countries said that they would no longer buy hyacinth macaws. But even so, the macaws were not safe. People kept trapping them and smuggling them out of Brazil to those countries that would buy them. This still goes on today, although not as much as before. Conservationists believe that about 3000 hyacinth macaws are left in the wild. There used to be far more.

Two hyacinth macaws playing in a tree in the Pantanal area of Brazil. Of the 3000 hyacinth macaws remaining, more live in this area of savanna and forest than anywhere else.

11

A hyacinth macaw gnaws on a pebble. Parrots need to chew on hard material to stop their bills from becoming overgrown. The parrot is cradling the pebble in its left foot. A study has shown that many parrots are left-footed.

As we have seen, the hyacinth macaw is a bird of the forest. There is another blue macaw – Lear's macaw – that lives in a completely different type of **habitat**. Lear's macaw resembles the hyacinth in color but is only three quarters of its size. For over 100 years, trappers had been selling this macaw to parrot collectors, but they never said exactly where it came from. Scientists were curious. They believed it probably lived in Brazil, and so they went to look for it in the wild.

Brazil is a huge country, and parts of it have hardly been explored. The search for Lear's macaw began in 1964 and lasted until 1978. A team of scientists finally discovered the macaw in a part of northeast Brazil that is little known to outsiders. It is not a forest area but a hot, dry, rocky place, covered with low, thorny plants. The team could hardly believe their eyes when they saw a small flock of Lear's macaws in front of them. For weeks they studied the birds. They found that there were about 60 of them living in holes in the walls of a canyon. The team watched the birds climbing the rock, using their powerful bill as an extra foot.

Each morning, the scientists noted, the birds flew off to feed on palm nuts. Local people had cut down many palms

Many of the large trees inside which hyacinth macaws nest have been cut down to create cattle pasture. Ranchers have now decided to leave some standing. Not only does this help the macaws, but people pay to stay at the ranches and see the parrots in the wild.

13

North Atlantic Ocean

Equator

SOUTH AMERICA

BRAZIL

to make way for fields, so the birds had to travel huge distances to find food. This gave hunters the chance to kill the birds as they passed overhead. Like many macaws, Lear's have long been eaten by local people.

Probably only 60 Lear's macaws survive in the wild. In 1992, the World Parrot Trust started the "Palm for a Parrot" fund to pay for the planting of palms near the parrots' home. It is hoped this will help solve the macaw's food shortage. However, Lear's macaw is also in danger from trappers. Because it is so rare, people will pay a lot for it. Part of the macaw's range happens to lie inside a **reserve**. Conservationists have asked that this protected area be enlarged to take in more of the bird's home. If enough habitat can be saved and the trappers kept away, Lear's macaw may survive. But it will be a close-run race.

Lear's macaw perched in a tree. Note how it grasps the branch. Most birds place three toes in front and the fourth behind. Parrots, like woodpeckers, put two toes in front and two behind.

New Zealand Parrots

New Zealand is home to seven parrots that are found nowhere else in the world. These include the kakapo, which is the world's only flightless parrot. The kakapo can leap and glide for a few feet but it cannot actually fly. The bird's breast muscles are too weak to keep it in the air. This is not surprising since the kakapo is also the world's heaviest parrot, with males weighing as much as 8 pounds (3.6 kg). A fully grown hyacinth macaw does not weigh even half that amount!

The kakapo is really a very unusual parrot. Most parrots are social birds, but the kakapo is solitary. Parrots are

The kakapo prefers to live in forests and woods. Since it cannot fly, the kakapo builds its nest on the ground – among tree roots, for example.

15

usually active during the day, but the kakapo comes out at night. Aside from its bill, the kakapo doesn't even look much like a parrot. It has a round face like an owl, whiskers like a cat, and dull-colored feathers of green, black, brown, and yellow.

Perhaps the most extraordinary thing about the kakapo is the male's strange call at breeding time. This is his way of finding a female. The call is a "booming" noise much like the sound you make when you blow across the top of a large, empty, glass bottle. A male can make 1000 "booms" an hour and may call all night long without stopping! Eventually, a female visits him, they **mate**, and the female goes away to lay her eggs and bring up the chicks alone.

Because of its round face, the kakapo is sometimes called the owl parrot. In the language of New Zealand's Maori people, "kakapo" means "parrot of the dark."

Until about 1000 years ago, the birds and animals had New Zealand to themselves. There were no meat-eating **mammals**, so kakapos were not in danger on the ground. Then people arrived. Suddenly everything changed. People hunted parrots for food as did the animals they brought with them – such as cats and dogs. The kakapos were not used to such dangerous enemies. They couldn't fight them, nor could they escape, because they were unable to fly. To make matters worse, people also brought plant-eating animals, such as deer, to New Zealand. These eat the same food as kakapos, and scientists believe they may have caused them to starve in some places.

By the 1970s, there were hardly any kakapos left. A small number survived on New Zealand's South Island, but

A kakapo bites into an apple. These birds eat all kinds of plant food and often chew leaves without taking them off the plant. Chewed leaves are a good sign that a kakapo has been in the area.

all of them were males. Scientists had almost given up hope of saving the bird, when, in 1977, some males and females were found on Stewart Island, off the coast of South Island. Unfortunately, the island's cats had also found them. However, conservationists came up with an answer. They caught the surviving birds and moved them to other islands where there were no cats. In 1994, there were almost 50 kakapos living in safety on these islands. Conservationists believe they may have saved this unusual parrot from becoming extinct.

The kakapo is not the only strange parrot found in New Zealand. The kea, which lives high in the mountains of

Areas where the kakapo (red) and kea (brown) can be found

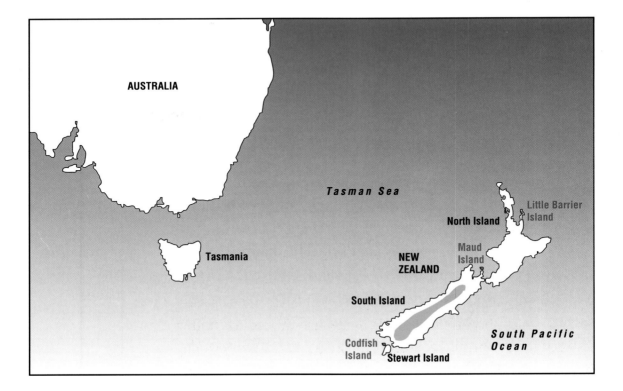

Keas live in the mountains in wooded river valleys, beech woods, and on highland grasslands. They can withstand cold weather, and on sunny winter days they can be seen rolling in the snow.

South Island, is a meat-eating parrot! During the summer, it feeds on fruit and other plant food. But in winter, the mountains are covered with snow and there is little to eat. At this time of year, keas are seen rummaging in garbage and searching ski lodges for scraps of food. They are fearless and intelligent and have been known to find their way into buildings by coming down the chimney.

The kea's habits got it into trouble with farmers. Farmers came across keas feeding on dead sheep. These parrots look a little like birds of prey. They are about 20 inches (50 cm) long, brownish with red under their wings, and heavy-set. They have fiercely hooked bills, too. People believed that the birds were killing their animals and started to hunt them. Many, many keas died. During the 1940s, nearly 7000 were killed in just three years. In truth, keas attack live sheep only rarely. They land on the animal's back at night and peck through its skin to feed on the layer of fat beneath. This does not kill the sheep, but the animal may panic and run over a cliff in the dark. More often, keas feed on animals that they find already dead from sickness or the cold. It is now illegal to hunt keas, and the bird is not in immediate danger of becoming extinct.

A kea chews at the rubber around the windshield of a car. It may be trying to get into the vehicle or just checking if the rubber can be eaten.

Areas where the
thick-billed parrot
can be found

Thick-billed Parrot

The thick-billed parrot lives in Mexico and in parts of the southwestern United States and makes its home in highland pine forests. We think of parrots as birds of warm places, yet high up in the mountains, winter temperatures may drop very low. It can even snow. Like the kea, the thick-billed parrot is able to withstand the cold.

Thick-billed parrots feed on pine nuts, which is why they need such a thick, strong beak. When they feed, they use the bill first as a powerful nutcracker to split open the pine cones. Then it becomes a deft pair of tweezers for tugging the tiny nuts from their shell.

A pair of thick-billed parrots. As is the case with most species of parrots, male and female thick-bills look the same.

21

A thick-billed parrot stretches its wings and shows off their beautiful color.

The thick-billed parrot is 16 inches (40 cm) long and is bright green in color with flashes of red. It sounds as if it should be easy to spot, and it is when it comes out into the open. Most of the time, though, it stays deep in its forest home, and even the brightest-colored birds are hard to see in the woods. However, if you cannot see the thick-billed parrot you can nearly always hear it. Thick-billed parrots move around the forest in flocks, looking for food. As they go, they squawk and chatter to one another all the time.

At one time, the thick-billed parrot's range stretched all the way from the Sierra Madre mountains in Mexico, north into New Mexico and Arizona. In the early years of the twentieth century, flocks could be huge. A group of miners in the Chiricahua Mountains, Arizona, reported seeing a flock of 700-1000 birds. By about 1935, however, thick-billed parrots were no longer spotted in the United States.

One reason for the bird's disappearance was that people had shot huge numbers of thick-billed parrots for food. Another was that they had cut down large areas of pine forest in the southwestern United States. Scientists believe that thick-billed parrots wander from area to area in search of food and nest trees. With few trees left in Arizona and New Mexico, the birds stopped traveling into the United States. In the meantime, the Mexicans started cutting down their forests for timber, too. Sadly, much parrot habitat has now disappeared.

Thick-billed parrots were also trapped to be sold as pets. They are still being captured in the 1990s, even though the

A thick-billed parrot cleans its mate. Paying each other attention like this helps the pair to build a close relationship.

bird is on the CITES list. CITES stands for the Convention on International Trade in Endangered Species. It is an international agreement in which more than 100 countries say that they will not buy or sell the endangered animals on the list. However, people break the law and smuggle thick-billed parrots. In 1986, the United States authorities discovered about 30 birds that people were trying to smuggle from Mexico. Conservationists released these into the wild in the Chiricahua Mountains and kept a close watch on them. Since then, young birds have been seen in Arizona. It seems that the thick-billed parrot has returned to American skies.

Through the efforts of conservation organizations, thick-billed parrots are once again feeding in the pine forests of Arizona.

ST. LUCIA

Caribbean Sea

SOUTH AMERICA

Area where the St Lucia parrot can be found

The St Lucia parrot is mainly green with a bluish face, a red throat, a reddish breast and belly, and blue and red patches on its wings.

St Lucia Parrot

The Amazons are a group of heavy-set parrots that measure up to 16 inches (40 cm) in length. They are mainly green but have flashes of bright colors, too. About 25 species of Amazons exist and each has its own distinct pattern.

A captive St Lucia parrot enjoys a meal. In 1979, the island's government made the St Lucia parrot the national bird.

The group is named after the Amazon region of South America, where many of these birds live. However, a number of Amazons live on the many tiny islands that lie in the Caribbean Sea. No less than five of these island Amazons are in danger, including the St Lucia Amazon, often known simply as the St Lucia parrot.

St Lucia parrots spend their time in small, noisy groups. They are active during the morning and in the late afternoon and early evening, searching the forest for fruit, nuts, seeds, and berries. The parrots rest during the heat of the day and when it rains. Rainstorms can be heavy in St Lucia, and the parrots prefer to wait them out. When the rain stops, the birds become busier and noisier than ever. Then, as the sun starts to set, they return to their **roosts**, making one last flight around the area before they settle down for the night.

As a small island, St Lucia has never been home to very many Amazons. However, between the 1950s and the 1970s, their numbers fell from about 1000 to 150. In addition to being trapped to become pets, many St Lucia parrots were shot for food. Many forests in which the bird lived were also cut down. The parrot survived only in the mountain forest in the center of the island – about one sixth of its former range.

Just in time, experts and the people of St Lucia got together. In 1975, conservationists from the Wildlife Preservation Trust captured seven young St Lucia parrots. With the permission of the St Lucia government, they took them back to their base in Jersey, Britain, and set up a breeding program. This was done so that if all the wild birds died out, there would at least be some St Lucia parrots left in the world.

The "Jacquot Express," a bus provided by the World Parrot Trust. It tours St Lucia putting on exhibitions about parrots and the forest. Jacquot (pronounced "Jacko") is the local name for the St Lucia parrot.

In the meantime, the St Lucia government made it illegal to hunt or trap St Lucia parrots or to take them from the island. Reserves were set up, and some parrot habitat was even replanted. The forest department started a campaign to teach the St Lucian people about their parrot. Parrot posters were sent to schools, and signs were put up by the roadside. All starred a parrot called "Jacquot," who told people how to look after the environment. For example, one sign read: "Jacquot says … help preserve a beautiful scene, keep St Lucia nice and clean; don't drop litter."

The St Lucia parrot is a conservation success story. Between 300 and 350 St Lucia parrots now live in the wild. The population is growing, and the St Lucians are determined to look after their national birds.

A baby St Lucia parrot born in Jersey, Britain. By 1989, 16 St Lucia parrots had been raised there. Two of these have now been returned to St Lucia and may one day be released into the wild.

Saving parrots is a very tough job. The forests where many parrots live are being cut down. This is unlikely to stop immediately. These forests are often in poor countries that need to sell timber to make money. Also, parrots are still trapped to be sold as pets and hunted for food.

But in a number of countries, people are learning to see the importance of their wildlife. They have passed laws against trapping and hunting parrots and are trying hard to make people obey them. Patches of parrot habitat have been set aside and even replanted, so the birds can feed and nest. As a result, some endangered parrots are on the way to being saved. Others need help now before it is too late.

The St Vincent parrot is another of the Caribbean Amazons at risk. Like the St Lucia parrot, it is being helped, and its story may have a happy ending.

Useful Addresses

For more information about parrots and how you can help protect them, contact these organizations:

Conservation International
1015 18th Street NW
Washington, D.C. 20036

National Audubon Society
950 Third Avenue
New York, N.Y. 10022

National Wildlife Federation
1400 16th Street NW
Washington, D.C. 20036

U.S. Fish and Wildlife Service
Endangered Species and Habitat
Conservation
400 Arlington Square
18th and C Streets NW
Washington, D.C. 20240

Wildlife Preservation Trust Canada
56 The Esplanade, Ste 205
Toronto ON M5E 1A7

Wildlife Preservation Trust International
3400 Girard Avenue
Philadelphia, PA 19104

World Wildlife Fund
1250 24th Street NW
Washington, D.C. 20037

Further Reading

African Gray Parrots Annette Wolter (Hauppauge, NY: Barron's, 1987)

Amazing Tropical Birds Gerald Legg (New York: Knopf, 1991)

The Bird Atlas Barbara Taylor (New York: Dorling Kindersley, 1993)

Endangered Wildlife of the World (New York: Marshall Cavendish Corporation, 1993)

Parrots Peter Murray (Plymouth, MN: Child's World, 1993)

Parrots Wildlife Education Staff (San Diego: Wildlife Education, 1984)

Saving Endangered Birds: Ensuring a Future In the Wild Thane Maynard (New York: Franklin Watts, 1993)

Wildlife of the World (New York: Marshall Cavendish Corporation, 1994)

Glossary

Adapt: To change in order to survive in new conditions.

Bird of prey: A type of bird that usually has a hooked bill and clawed feet and hunts and eats other animals.

Captive: Kept in confinement; for parrots, usually in a cage.

Conservationist (Kon-ser-VAY-shun-ist): A person who protects and preserves the Earth's natural resources, such as animals, plants, and soil.

Extinct (Ex-TINKT): No longer living anywhere in the world.

Family: A group of animal species. For example, the parrot family.

Habitat: The place where an animal lives. For example, the scarlet macaw's habitat is the rainforest.

Mammal: A kind of animal that is warm-blooded and has a backbone. Most are covered with fur or have hair. Females have glands that produce milk to feed their young.

Mate: 1) An animal's partner, with which it breeds; 2) When a male and female get together to produce young.

Rainforest: A forest that has heavy rainfall much of the year.

Range: The area in the world in which a particular species of animal can be found.

Reserve: Land that has been set aside where plants and animals can live without being harmed.

Roost: A place where a bird sleeps. For a parrot, this might be inside a tree or a hole in a cliff.

Savanna: Wide open plains found in tropical parts of the world. Grass is the main type of plant, and trees are few and widely scattered.

Species: A kind of animal or plant. For example, the scarlet macaw and the thick-billed parrot are two different species of parrots.

Tropical: Having to do with or found in the tropics, the warm region of the Earth near the Equator. For example, tropical rainforest.

Index